WORLD'S SCARIEST PRISONS

EMMA
CARLSON
BERNE

SCHOLASTIC INC.

Copyright © 2014 Scholastic Inc.

All rights reserved. Published by Scholastic Inc. SCHOLASTIC and associated logos are trademarks and/or registered trademarks of Scholastic Inc.

ISBN 978-545-68023-3

12 11 10 9 8 7 6 5 4 3   14 15 16 17 18 19

Printed in the U.S.A. 40

First printing, September 2014

Designed by Liz Herzog and Kay Petronio

CONTENTS

Introduction. 4

The Roman Colosseum 6

Fleet Prison. 12

The Tower of London 18

The Bastille. 24

Elmina Castle 30

Carandiru Penitentiary 36

Robben Island 40

Public Gaol 46

Livingston's Sugar House 50

Burlington County Prison 54

Eastern State Penitentiary. 58

Devil's Island. 62

Fremantle Prison 68

Ohio State Reformatory 74

Squirrel Cage Jail. 78

Kolyma Gulag Camp. 82

Alcatraz. 88

Hoa Lo Prison 94

Attica 98

Sing Sing. 104

Glossary 110

INTRODUCTION

SLAMMER.
BIG HOUSE.
JOINT.
CLINK.

PRISON—where criminals spend long days, removed from society, as punishment for their **CRIMES**.

These are the prisons of today. In much of history, however, prison served an altogether different purpose. Prisons and jails were places that held people awaiting either their trial or their execution. Locking someone up as **PUNISHMENT** hadn't been thought of yet.

Now, the government pays to clothe and feed their prisoners. In the past, prisoners had to pay for their own food and bring their own clothing. If a prisoner didn't have money to pay for food, he either starved or was fed the smallest amount to keep him alive. When his clothes became tattered, he wore the rags or went naked. Prisons were often wet, dark, and terribly crowded.

In the early nineteenth century, some scholars argued that prison could be a punishment all on its own. They suggested that people who committed crimes might be capable of change. If they could be placed in a crime-free environment, perhaps they could REFORM themselves. Gradually, "going to prison" became an accepted punishment.

This was the beginning of the modern prison system.

THE ROMAN COLOSSEUM

The Roman Colosseum was a giant, magnificent arena that could hold fifty thousand spectators. Underneath the arena were cells that held gladiators waiting to fight. Construction of the Colosseum began in the first century CE under the rule of Emperor Vespasian. Its **GRAND** design served a specific purpose: Vespasian wanted it to express how powerful he was as a ruler. (Hint: He was very powerful.)

BEHIND THE BARS

ALSO KNOWN AS:	the Colosseum or Coliseum, the Flavian Amphitheatre
LOCATED IN:	Rome, Italy
OPERATIONAL:	80 CE until the sixth century
NUMBER OF PRISONERS:	There were enough cells to hold the gladiators competing that day—as well as some wild animals—and space for an estimated 50,000 spectators.
NOTABLE INMATES:	famous gladiators like Flamma, Priscus, and Verus

Elaborate spectacles were staged there, such as reenactments of entire sea battles, where the arena was filled with water and wooden warships. Yet much of what passed for entertainment in ancient Rome was truly gruesome. **CRIMINALS** were publicly executed at the Colosseum. Slaves and criminals were sent into the arena to engage in **BATTLES TO THE DEATH** with wild animals.

INSIDE THE ARENA

BATTLE TIME

The most notorious events were the **BATTLES OF GLADIATORS**, which often ended in the death of one of the fighters. So much blood was spilled that the sand on the arena floor was dyed red to mask the gory sight. Some gladiators were volunteers who were free to come and go as they wanted. Other gladiators were **PRISONERS** or slaves. They were sent against their will to participate in the *ludi*, or public games, and were trained in the gladiatorial arts in special schools.

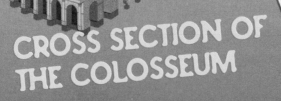

CROSS SECTION OF THE COLOSSEUM

LIFE IN PRISON

The gladiators were important to the owners who organized their fights, so they received the best diet, fitness training, and medical care available. From examining gladiator remains, scientists have been able to tell that the gladiators ate a lot of carbohydrates, like barley, beans, and peas. This food was supposed to make the gladiator gain weight—a layer of fat would protect him from flesh wounds during the battle. And when gladiators survived their fights, their wounds were treated expertly.

When it came time for their fights, the gladiators might travel through an underground passageway directly to dungeons beneath the Colosseum, where they would be locked in cells alongside lions, tigers, bears, and elephants. There they waited to hear when and how they would fight, and wondered whether they would leave the arena alive.

After several hundred years of battles and games, the Colosseum fell into disrepair from **FIRE, EARTHQUAKES,** and **LOOTING.** During medieval times, people planted vegetable gardens and dumped waste in the basement. Gradually, the dungeons under the Colosseum **DECAYED.** The Colosseum remained in that state until Benito Mussolini, the prime minister of Italy, ordered its excavation in the 1930s. Today, the dungeons under the Colosseum are open again. Tourists come from near and far to walk those same stones, imagining, perhaps, the terrifying **RUMBLE OF BATTLES ABOVE.**

PASSAGEWAYS WHERE GLADIATORS ONCE WALKED

GLADIATOR BATTLES

The word *gladiator* brings images of **WARRIORS** entering arenas to great cheers. Famous gladiators were the celebrities of Roman society. Gladiator battles were very popular— all classes of Romans attended, with the nobility watching from a special box right near the action.

To prepare to fight, a gladiator usually wore only a tunic or a loincloth held up by a metal belt. He might wear shin guards and a helmet made of bronze. The gladiator carried a large shield and a spear, lance, or sword. Some gladiators entered the arena on horseback and then dismounted to fight. Sometimes they would battle accompanied by music. If the loser of the fight was not killed during the battle, then the audience might decide his fate by giving a thumbs-up sign—which meant he must be executed on the spot by the winner.

The winner would receive prizes: a palm branch, money, and perhaps a wreath of laurel, which was a sign of honor. To complete the spectacle, the **WINNING GLADIATOR** would run a lap around the arena, waving his palm branch.

A gladiator might fight only three times a year and could expect to die either in battle or from his wounds by the age of about twenty-seven. This might seem very young, but the late twenties was the average life expectancy for most Roman people.

FLEET PRISON

Imagine walking a London street in the late eighteenth century. A massive stone building crowds the sidewalk. From inside, sobbing voices cry out, **"ALMS! ALMS!"** Hands reach from barred windows, plucking at your coat. Alarmed, you fumble in your pocket for a few coins to deposit into a little box fixed to the front of a cell.

BEHIND THE BARS

ALSO KNOWN AS: Fleet Debtors' Prison

LOCATED IN: London, England, by the Fleet River

OPERATIONAL: 1197–1842

NUMBER OF PRISONERS: Up to 300 debtors and their families were imprisoned at a time.

NOTABLE INMATES: JOHN DONNE (poet), BEN JONSON (playwright), SIR WALTER RALEIGH (explorer, writer), SIR THOMAS LODGE (lord mayor of London), JØRGEN JØRGENSEN (Danish adventurer)

This is **FLEET PRISON**, which operated near the Fleet River from 1197 until it was closed by an act of Parliament in 1842, during Queen Victoria's reign. People who owed financial debts were the first prisoners in Fleet, but before long, prisoners of all kinds were sent there.

WHO DID TIME?

JOHN DONNE

The population expanded to include **PROTESTORS**, **REBELS**, and **POLITICAL** and **RELIGIOUS PRISONERS**. The poet John Donne and the philosopher and religious rebel William Penn—later the founder of the colonial province of Pennsylvania—are just two of many historical and literary figures who did time at Fleet.

Conditions at Fleet Prison were actually somewhat **BETTER** than at other prisons of this era—at least if you had enough money. Wealthy debtors lived on one side of the prison, where they had their own **ROOMS** and **FURNITURE**, and **SERVANTS** to wait on them.

Prisoners could pay the warden for better food and for outings. And if a prisoner had enough money, he or she could even pay to live outside the prison walls.

Life at Fleet was very different if you were poor. As in many debtors' prisons, poor prisoners were crowded together, often chained, and left covered in **FILTH**. There are records of prisoners being forced to **EAT WITH HOGS** in the same space, and of people being so starved, they caught and ate mice. A bishop imprisoned there described his bed as "a little pad of straw, with a **ROTTEN** covering."

PRISON CONDITIONS

The conditions at Fleet were very **DIRTY**. At one point, raw sewage from the prison was choking the portion of the Fleet River that ran by the prison. Prisoners became sick, and authorities were forced to investigate.

Fleet Prison was finally demolished in 1846. Farringdon Street runs over the site where the Fleet once was. No trace remains of the prison that stood for nearly seven hundred years.

FARRINGDON STREET IN 1900

DEBTORS' PRISONS

If a business or person lends you money in today's world and you don't pay it back on time, that person can take you to court. He can take some of the wages you earn. Or he can make it hard for you to borrow money in the future. But none of these punishments are as bad as being **THROWN IN PRISON**. And that's exactly what would happen to you until the early nineteenth century if you borrowed money and didn't pay it back in England and other countries.

Your creditor—the person to whom you owe money—could order you to be sent to prison. And there you would stay, for sentences as short as a few days or as long as many years. Debtors' prisons were a for-profit business. If you had money, you could pay the warden—the head jailer—for better food and for your own room. Of course, the problem with debtors' prisons, many scholars pointed out, was this: How could a debtor repay his debt if he was **IMPRISONED** and could not work or otherwise get money to pay back his debts?

THE TOWER OF LONDON

The Tower of London is not only a tower but a **MASSIVE COMPLEX** of buildings and grounds. Begun by William the Conqueror in the 1070s as a fortress, the original Tower was completed in 1100, and the rest of the compound by 1350.

BEHIND THE BARS

ALSO KNOWN AS: Her Majesty's Royal Palace and Fortress

LOCATED IN: London, England, along the Thames River

OPERATIONAL: 1100–1952

NUMBER OF PRISONERS: More than 8,000 over the centuries

NOTABLE INMATES: ELIZABETH I (Queen of England), ANNE BOLEYN (second wife of Henry VIII), THOMAS CROMWELL (chief minister to Henry VIII), SIR WALTER RALEIGH (explorer, writer), GUY FAWKES (planned the Gunpowder Plot)

BIRDS-EYE VIEW OF TOWER

It had been used by England's monarchs as a royal residence, a storage center for valuable papers, and an area for victory parties. It was not until the sixteenth-century rule of Henry VIII that the Tower became a prison.

NOT YOUR AVERAGE CRIMINALS

This was no place for common criminals; it was instead reserved for **elite** prisoners such as wealthy nobles and anyone who threatened the power of the throne. The politician Sir Thomas More, as well as the English prince Edward V, not to mention two of Henry VIII's own wives, Anne Boleyn and Catherine Howard, were **EXECUTED** at the Tower! It was also common for people whose religious beliefs challenged those of the monarch to be sent to the Tower. Even Elizabeth I was sent there (by her own half sister, Queen Mary!) in 1554 before she became queen four years later. She, too, would send political and religious rebels to the Tower during her long reign as queen.

WARDERS AT THE TOWER

LIFE IN THE TOWER

Living out the rest of your days at the Tower, waiting to be executed, must have been horrible. But daily life in the Tower wasn't all bad. Accommodations were **SPACIOUS**, and noble prisoners entertained friends and family with food and drink served by their own staff. Sir Walter Raleigh brought his family with him to the Tower, and received treatment from his own doctors there. King John of France was even permitted to travel the country while technically a prisoner in the Tower. At one point, he gave a **FEAST** that included twelve chickens and dozens of bottles of wine.

EXECUTIONS

Even though some prisoners were held in nice accomodations, the Tower was also a site of gruesome **TORTURE** and execution. Many prisoners were **BEHEADED** right in the Tower's courtyard, executions that were public events for anyone who wanted to attend. Perhaps the most famous person beheaded at the Tower was **ANNE BOLEYN**, who in 1536 was convicted of **CRIMES** against her husband, **THE KING**. Due to Anne's royal status, Henry VIII brought in an expert executioner from France to do the job.

KING HENRY VIII WITH ANNE BOLEYN

GHOSTS IN THE TOWER OF LONDON

In 1610, Arabella Stuart, a descendant of Henry VII, was imprisoned in the Queen's House, a building on the grounds of the Tower of London. She married without permission of the king, which was not allowed in those days. When King James discovered her marriage, he ordered her to be imprisoned in the Tower. Arabella died in the Tower in 1615. The Queen's House is now a residence, and guests who have stayed in Arabella's room have woken in the night feeling the tight grip of someone's hands on their throat. But no one is ever there—except, perhaps, the **GHOST OF ARABELLA**.

Another story tells of a bear that reportedly has haunted the Martin Tower, where the Crown Jewels are displayed today. Two bears have lived at the Tower of London in the past: a polar bear that was given as a gift to Henry III from the king of Norway in 1251, and a grizzly bear from North America, given by the Hudson Bay Company to George III in 1811. A **GHOSTLY BEAR**—perhaps the ghost of one of these bears—supposedly appeared many years ago in the Tower. Legend has it that it shocked a guard so badly, the man died from fright.

THE BASTILLE

On July 14, 1789, a **MOB** of angry French citizens surrounded the mighty stone walls of the Bastille. This fortress, built in the fourteenth century, was a political prison. To the revolutionary people seeking to overthrow the monarchy, the Bastille had become a symbol of the monarchy's unjust rule.

BEHIND THE BARS

ALSO KNOWN AS:	Bastille Saint-Antoine
LOCATED IN:	Paris, France
OPERATIONAL:	1417 until the French Revolution in 1789
NUMBER OF PRISONERS:	More than 5,000 inmates had been held in the Bastille by the time it was destroyed.
NOTABLE INMATES:	CHARLES GONTAUT (Duke of Biron), VOLTAIRE (author), MARQUIS DE SADE (philosopher and writer), MARGUERITE DE LAUNAY (author)

The revolutionaries believed that the French monarchs were **dictators** who could imprison people whenever they wanted—and the Bastille was proof.

THE FRENCH FLAG

The mob broke into the building, looking for gunpowder stored there. They were also looking for the prison governor. The mob found, killed, and beheaded him, and also **SET FREE** seven prisoners.

This event is considered to mark the start of the **French Revolution.** Soon after the end of the war, the story of the Bastille began to shift. Writers portrayed the **STORMING OF THE BASTILLE,** as it came to be called, as a story of **liberation,** while in truth it all started as a search for ammunition. Famed authors like Victor Hugo and Alexandre Dumas wrote popular stories about prisoners held for decades in the dungeons of the Bastille, men who did not see the light of day for years. These stories were very popular among the French people.

THE TRUTH

The **REALITY** of life in the Bastille was different than the stories. Compared to other eighteenth-century French prisons, scholars suggest, conditions were bearable. In fact, **DUNGEONS** in the Bastille were barely in use at the time of the siege. Many of the prisoners in the Bastille were political figures who could pay for food, medical care, and warm baths. The writer Marquis de Sade brought rugs and wine with him. The philosopher Voltaire had so many visitors that authorities were forced to limit his guests to five or six per day. Even after his sentence ended, Voltaire stayed at the Bastille to finish up some business.

VOLTAIRE AT THE BASTILLE

DESTRUCTION

Ultimately, the massive fortress was **DESTROYED** during the French Revolution, and only a few stones remain to mark its spot on the Place de la Bastille. But the Storming of the Bastille is still observed annually as a **NATIONAL HOLIDAY** in France on July 14.

PLACE DE LA BASTILLE, WHERE THE BASTILLE ONCE STOOD

OUBLIETTES AT THE BASTILLE

The oubliette has been compared to the "chokey," a device described in Roald Dahl's *Matilda*. These torture chambers were **RUMORED** to exist at the Bastille and were definitely in use at other prisons. The prisoner was thrown or lowered on a rope into a narrow, tube-shaped, underground dungeon. Its only opening was at the top, through which guards tossed food to the prisoners. Sometimes the oubliette would fill with water; some were too narrow for prisoners to comfortably sit or lie down. The word *oubliette* comes from the French verb *oublier*, which means **"TO FORGET."**

ELMINA CASTLE

When Africans were forcibly torn from their homeland to become slaves in what was known as the **"NEW WORLD,"** they were often first held as prisoners at Elmina Castle. It was the last they would ever see of their continent.

BEHIND THE BARS

ALSO KNOWN AS:	São Jorge da Mina Castle
LOCATED IN:	Elmina, Ghana
OPERATIONAL:	1482 until 1872 when the British took over the fort after the Dutch abolished the slave trade
NUMBER OF PRISONERS:	More than 30,000 prisoners passed through Elmina per year at its peak.
NOTABLE INMATES:	The king of an African city was imprisoned at Elmina during 1896–1897 after the British took control.

Elmina was the first permanent structure built by Europeans in Africa, south of the Sahara desert. It was also the first permanent **SLAVE** outpost. Constructed in Ghana in 1492, it still **TOWERS** over the sand and water at the far western African coast.

IMPRISONMENT

INTERIOR CELL

Elmina was originally a gold-trading post, but by the 1600s the Dutch were using it to imprison Africans. The massive building's upstairs housed European **SLAVE TRADERS**, who slept on beds in comfortably furnished suites. Downstairs, recently **CAPTURED** Africans were crowded into horrific **DUNGEONS** to await their fate as slaves. Sometimes, up to two hundred people occupied one cell, leaving no room to lie down; all had to sit or stand.

A SKULL AND CROSSBONES MARKS THE ENTRANCE TO A SLAVE CELL

SLAVES AT ELMINA

Slave traders captured people across the continent and traded them for objects like shells, guns, knives, bars of iron, silk, or mirrors. Then they were forced to **MARCH TO THE COAST**. Many died along the way. Those who survived were held in Elmina's cells until a ship arrived to transport them **ACROSS THE ATLANTIC**.

Elmina's location on the very edge of the coast was no accident. The castle gave sea captains a safe place to load their ships in the harbor, since pirate attacks were a constant threat.

DOOR OF NO RETURN

Upon leaving Elmina Castle, slaves walked through the **DOOR OF NO RETURN**, a small opening in the castle walls. Rowboats took chained slaves to the big ships. By the 1700s, more than thirty thousand people were sent through that door each year.

Today, Elmina still stands. It is a UNESCO World Heritage Site, a museum, a monument, and a concrete reminder of a **TERRIBLE PERIOD** in world history.

THE MIDDLE PASSAGE

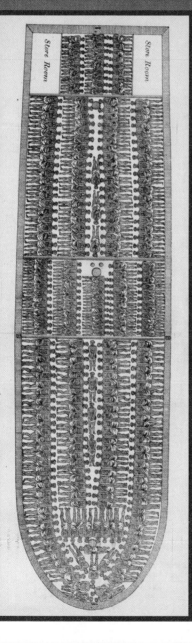

Africans leaving Elmina Castle on slave ships left one prison only to find themselves once more in another. Conditions on the ships were even more horrific than those at the slave posts. Passengers were packed together with little room to move, and endured **UNTHINKABLY BRUTAL** living conditions. The ship captains considered their human passengers to be "cargo" and wanted the African prisoners to arrive alive so that they could be sold. Even so, many died at sea. The ocean crossing would last from two to four months, and in this time an estimated twenty percent of the people on board died from sickness and the **INHUMANE CONDITIONS**.

CARANDIRU PENITENTIARY

At its peak, Carandiru Penitentiary was the **LARGEST** prison on the South American continent. The vast complex in São Paulo, Brazil, opened in 1956, was built to house up to four thousand people. Its population later grew to more than eight thousand

BEHIND THE BARS

ALSO KNOWN AS:	Estação Carandiru (or Carandiru Station)
LOCATED IN:	São Paulo, Brazil
OPERATIONAL:	1956–2002
NUMBER OF PRISONERS:	Housed more than 8,000 inmates at its peak
NOTABLE INMATES:	During a large prison riot in 1992, 111 inmates were killed and another 87 were injured, and a movie was based on the event.

THE VIEW FROM OUTSIDE A CELL

The prisoners at Carandiru were so terribly overcrowded that ten men might be **SQUEEZED** into a cell that was meant for one or two. They were not permitted sunlight or fresh air.

Carandiru's abuses and overcrowding created tension among prisoners that **BOILED OVER** on October 2, 1992. Later reports described a fight between two prisoners that set off fighting between rival **PRISON GANGS**. Police tried to get the rebellion under control, but the situation only worsened. Police were later accused of committing unjust violent acts against the rioting prisoners.

Eleven hours later, when the **RIOT** was finally over, more than one hundred prisoners lay dead, but no officers had been killed. After the "Carandiru Massacre," twenty-five police officers were sentenced to over six hundred years in prison for their role in the riot.

Then more violence erupted in 2002. Inmates with cell phones coordinated riots at twenty-seven jails across the country and held thousands of visitors **HOSTAGE**. Carandiru was shut down shortly afterward, leaving behind a bloody history.

UNDERSTANDING PRISON GANGS

Prison gangs are groups of prisoners who band together to support one another, and sometimes commit **CRIMINAL ACTS**. Prison gangs can be a threat to prison peace because they are often violent and have been linked to the prison drug trade. Like gangs in non-prison life, prison gangs are often strictly organized, with leaders, junior leaders, and upper- and lower-level members. Gangs often wear identifying items, and use code words or gestures that distinguish them from other gangs. The Aryan Brotherhood, for instance, is a violent prison gang that supports racist beliefs and actions linked to white supremacy.

The Barrio Azteca is a very large, mostly Mexican and Mexican American prison gang known for smuggling drugs into prisons. Their symbols are *BA* and *21*, among others.

ROBBEN ISLAND

WE SERVE WITH PRIDE reads the sign over the entrance to the Robben Island prison. But the political prisoners held on this **ISOLATED, ROCKY ISLAND** off the coast of South Africa likely disagreed.

BEHIND THE BARS

ALSO KNOWN AS:	The Island
LOCATED IN:	Cape Town, South Africa
OPERATIONAL:	1961–1991
NUMBER OF PRISONERS:	More than 3,000 political activists while Robben Island functioned as a prison
NOTABLE INMATES:	NELSON MANDELA (Nobel Laureate, former president of South Africa), KGALEMA MOTLANTHE (former president of South Africa), JACOB ZUMA (current president of South Africa)

PRISON ENTRANCE

Robben Island has served different purposes over the years, as a leper colony and a military outpost. But during South Africa's era of **apartheid** (1948–1996), it served as a prison for activists who opposed the government's racial discrimination policies.

41

LIFE IN PRISON

Many prisoners were held for years, some for **DECADES**. Conditions on the island were infamously **HARSH**. Prisoners were kept in **TINY CELLS** and fed only porridge. Beatings and other brutal treatment by the guards were common. The most famous prisoner at Robben Island was **NELSON MANDELA**, the revolutionary, activist, Nobel Peace Prize winner, and former president of South Africa. Mandela worked to end the racist segregation practices of the apartheid government. He was **ARRESTED** and **ACCUSED** of trying to overthrow the government in 1962. He was sent to Robben Island where he was imprisoned from 1964 until 1982.

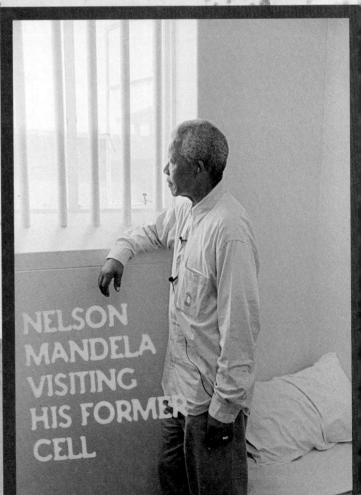

NELSON MANDELA VISITING HIS FORMER CELL

ALL ALONE

NELSON MANDELA'S CELL

Mandela was allowed only one visitor a year, who could stay for only thirty minutes. He was allowed to send one letter every six months.

For the prisoners, the **ISOLATION** was almost as **PAINFUL** as the living conditions. One of the only times inmates could communicate with one another was when emptying and cleaning their chamber pots in the mornings. In his autobiography, Mandela describes how the prisoners would try to whisper to one another in the evenings before they went to sleep. To do so, they would throw handfuls of sand on the floor outside their cells so they could hear the **FOOTSTEPS** of the guards approaching.

SECRET COMMUNICATION

In later years, conditions slightly improved. The **PRISONERS** were occasionally allowed to play tennis and other activities. Still, they had little time to communicate with one another. Sometimes they would cut open the tennis balls to **SLIP NOTES** inside and pass to a fellow prisoner.

GUARD TOWER AT ROBBEN ISLAND

WHAT IS A POLITICAL PRISONER?

Mahatma Gandhi, Leon Trotsky, Nelson Mandela, Eugene Debs, Aung San Suu Kyi. These very different people have one thing in common: Each was held as a political prisoner. A political prisoner is different from a criminal prisoner. A criminal goes to prison after being convicted of a specific crime—murder, for instance, or fraud. A political prisoner is **JAILED FOR WORDS** and **ACTIONS** that **CHALLENGE THE GOVERNMENT** or its policies. For example, political activists may be imprisoned if they try to overturn a government. The great Indian leader **MAHATMA GANDHI** was arrested and jailed many times in India, where he was working to free India from British rule. The British government thought Gandhi was dangerous because he encouraged Indian people to stand up for independence from colonial British rule.

PUBLIC GAOL

Several centuries ago, jails were often simple wooden sheds that were meant to hold people only for a short time, and from which prisoners could easily **ESCAPE**. But the Public Gaol (*gaol* is an early spelling of *jail*) in Williamsburg, Virginia, was one of the first **SECURE JAILS** in colonial America.

BEHIND THE BARS

ALSO KNOWN AS:	The Gaol
LOCATED IN:	Colonial Williamsburg, Virginia
OPERATIONAL:	1704–1910
NUMBER OF PRISONERS:	Countless runaway slaves, pirates, debtors, and mentally ill prisoners during its 200 years
NOTABLE INMATES:	FIFTEEN HENCHMEN OF THE PIRATE BLACKBEARD, HENRY "HAIR BUYER" HAMILTON (lieutenant governor of British Detroit)

BRICK PRISON

In the early 1700s, officials in Virginia's capital city ordered the construction of a "substantial brick prison."

WHO WERE THE INMATES?

When the jail was complete, debtors were locked away with runaway slaves and the mentally ill. During the American Revolution (1775–1783), political prisoners such as supporters of the British, spies, and traitors were locked in the Public Gaol. And in 1718, there were even some men who worked for the **PIRATE CAPTAIN BLACKBEARD**.

Conditions were crowded and unsanitary. **"JAIL FEVER,"** otherwise known as typhus, broke out often. There was no heat in the frigid Virginia winter, and most prisoners were chained at the hands and feet.

The Public Gaol was in use for the next two hundred years until 1910, when it was closed. It was later reopened, in 1936, as a part of historic Colonial Williamsburg.

PUBLIC PUNISHMENT METHOD OUTSIDE GAOL

PRISON SHIPS

Gaols on land weren't the only notorious prisons of the late eighteenth century. During the American Revolution, there were few empty buildings to house prisoners. So the British began keeping American prisoners of war in empty ships. Before long, sixteen **"PRISON SHIPS"** were filled with American revolutionaries captured in battle.

The conditions on the prison ships were particularly bad, even for the standards of the day. Prisoners were fed barely enough to keep them alive. Dead and dying prisoners were jammed together with healthy prisoners. **DISEASE** was everywhere. Depending on the season, prisoners spent sweltering or freezing days up on the deck, and brutal nights in the **CROWDED** lower levels of the ship. An American officer recalls being forced to sleep on cow dung without blankets or bedding, and being made to drink bilge water—the filthy water that collects in the bottom of a ship.

The suffering by American prisoners on Revolutionary-era prison ships was so extreme that a monument to them was erected in Brooklyn. The Prison Ship Martyrs Monument, a towering column, stands in Fort Greene Park, and the remains of 11,500 men and women who died on the ships rest in a grave beneath it.

LIVINGSTON'S SUGAR HOUSE

A Sugar House seems an odd place for a prison, but Livingston's Sugar House was a real jail, built in the 1770s in New York City. During this period, a **SUGAR HOUSE** was a warehouse for sugar and molasses that had been imported from the West Indies. These large, sturdy buildings

BEHIND THE BARS

LOCATED IN: Manhattan, New York

OPERATIONAL: 1754–1846

NUMBER OF PRISONERS: 400–500 inmates at a time

NOTABLE INMATES: Revolutionary War prisoners were held here, including JUDGE JOHN THOMAS and COMMODORE SILAS TALBOT (one of the first American naval commanders)

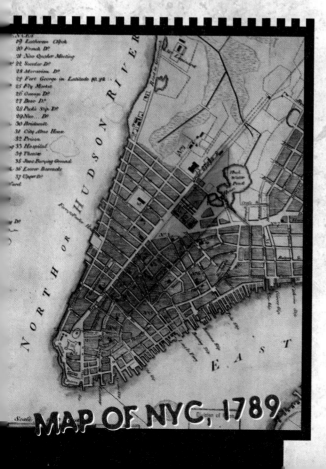

MAP OF NYC, 1789

But like so many prisons, Livingston's Sugar House was incredibly **OVERCROWDED**— four to five hundred prisoners were kept there, often in terrible living conditions. The prisoners were kept in near-starvation. One former prisoner wrote about his time in the Sugar House: A board fence encircled the dark, **GLOOMY BUILDING**, and windows were set high on the walls.

HUNGRY INMATES

Inside the walls were "emaciated, starving" men. They ate small amounts of pork and "sea biscuits." The biscuits were so **MOLDY** and wormy that prisoners had to boil them in water so the **WORMS** would float to the top. When they had fuel, inmates would also cook meat this way, but if no fuel was available, they would eat it raw. Stories were told of men who were so **HUNGRY**, they tried to eat their own clothes and shoes.

A SEA BISCUIT

PRISON FOOD

For most of history, prison food has been **FAMOUSLY BAD**. In the United States and Europe, moldy, stale bread and poorly cooked meat were ordinary prison fare. Fresh fruits and vegetables were too valuable to be wasted on prisoners. But often, throughout history, those who were wealthy and imprisoned could pay to receive better food—even wine to drink.

Today, prison food has been compared to medium-quality cafeteria food. In the United States, by law, prisoners **CANNOT BE STARVED** or deprived of nutrients as punishment. The food doesn't have to taste good, but there must be enough of it for health. And it must be edible. Prisoners are sometimes punished by being given a "nutraloaf" in place of their usual food—a blend of vegetables and potatoes mixed with dairy and processed chicken, shaped into a loaf, and baked. Not all prison food is bad. A menu from Alcatraz from the 1940s offers roast pork shoulder, chili, potato chowder, codfish, and apricot pie.

BURLINGTON COUNTY PRISON

The Burlington County Prison in New Jersey was built in 1811 with the dual purpose of holding prisoners and **rehabilitating** them. At that time, the idea that prisoners should be treated decently and could be taught to see the error of their ways was new.

BEHIND THE BARS

ALSO KNOWN AS:	Haunted Prison
LOCATED IN:	Mount Holly Township, New Jersey
OPERATIONAL:	1811–1965
NUMBER OF PRISONERS:	More than 100 inmates at a time
NOTABLE INMATES:	JOEL CLOUGH (whose ghost is said to haunt the prison!)

PRISON
ENTRANCE

Burlington County Prison was unique because it had ventilation, **FIREPLACES** in cells, a **GARDEN**, and **COMMON ROOMS**, all of which were installed for the prisoners' benefit. Inmates were bathed and deloused upon entry, and given a Bible.

Still, this *was* a prison, and prisoners were not happy to be there. Inmates tried to **ESCAPE** many times. During one escape in 1875, inmates hacked a hole in a corridor ceiling and made it out.

JOEL CLOUGH was not so successful. He was imprisoned in the massive stone building early in the nineteenth century. While awaiting sentencing, he managed to escape. He was caught and sent to a maximum-security cell known as the **DUNGEON**. In the dungeon, guards kept watch over the prisoners at all times. Clough was sentenced to death in 1833.

Soon after, inmates reported hearing **MOANS** and **RATTLING CHAINS**, and claimed to have seen **OBJECTS FLOATING** in midair. While the building was being restored in 1999, construction workers reported hearing loud voices and feeling wild temperature changes. Missing objects suddenly turned up in odd places.

The Burlington County Prison remained in use until 1965. Today it is a museum—and possibly the home of Joel Clough's **GHOST**.

CELL BLOCK

PRISONERS OR PENITENTS?

Before the nineteenth century, it was uncommon for prisoners to receive such basic rights as access to adequate food, shelter, and hygiene. Most people believed that convicted felons were **irredeemable** sinners. But early in the 1800s, reformers began to work on behalf of criminals. They believed it was society's job to see that prison inmates were fed and dressed, and not beaten or tortured. What's more, the reformers argued, it was possible to teach prisoners not to commit crimes again.

These ideas **revolutionized** the prison system. Inmates were no longer starved or tortured in state and county prisons. They were usually given adequate clothes and food, as well as access to toilets and sinks. But overcrowding and abuse from guards and wardens continues to be a problem in many prisons even today.

EASTERN STATE PENITENTIARY

After Eastern State Penitentiary (ESP) opened its doors in 1829, it became one of the most **FAMOUS PRISONS** in the world. It was one of the first true **"PENITENTIARIES,"** a place where prisoners could be taught to see the error of their ways.

BEHIND THE BARS

ALSO KNOWN AS:	ESP
LOCATED IN:	Philadelphia, Pennsylvania
OPERATIONAL:	1829–1971
NUMBER OF PRISONERS:	450 inmates at a time
NOTABLE INMATES:	WILLIE SUTTON (bank robber), AL CAPONE (gangster)

ENTRANCE TO THE CELL BLOCK

The inmates at ESP lived in silence and were not permitted to interact with one another or with the guards. They even had to **WEAR HOODS** over their heads when outside of their cells. If prisoners had time to **THINK** about their crimes, prison officials reasoned, they would come to **REGRET** their actions. This was later called the Pennsylvania system or the solitary system.

A NEW KIND OF PRISON

In the ESP cells, the prisoners had access to light only through a skylight and had a Bible and some amount of work or handicraft. Their meals were pushed into their cells through little doors. This focus on God and hard work was intended to help the prisoners regret their crimes.

Inmates at Eastern State were not beaten, tortured, or starved as prisoners had been during earlier eras. Furthermore, they had **RUNNING WATER, TOILETS, and CENTRAL HEAT** during a time when many people in society had no indoor plumbing and used coal-burning stoves for heat.

But the outside of the prison was designed to look scary and medieval, to appear intimidating. The interior was designed to look like a church, with arches, vaulted ceilings, and tall windows.

In later years, some common rooms were added, such as workshops and exercise yards. Yet the big prison was too expensive to maintain, and in 1971, it closed its doors forever.

AL CAPONE'S PRISON CELL

AL CAPONE, EASTERN STATE PENITENTIARY'S MOST NOTORIOUS PRISONER

After being arrested in 1929, the famed gangster Al Capone spent about one year at ESP. But he didn't exactly live in hardship. He furnished his cell with oil paintings, rugs, a radio, flowers, and even antique furniture. Other accounts argue that he was not given special treatment, that the LUXURY was overstated. But according to all accounts, "SCARFACE" was a model prisoner. He played handball and baseball with other prisoners, worked in the prison office, read books, and wrote letters. He was also something of a philanthropist, donating money to needy families. Newspaper accounts of the day reported that Capone sent money through the prison chaplain to poor families on the outside. He paid a woman's hospital bills and offered her husband a job. Capone was given two months off his sentence for GOOD BEHAVIOR. Years later, his bad behavior would land him in three other prisons.

DEVIL'S ISLAND

Just off the coast of South America, Devil's Island is one of three islands in French Guiana that make up the Îles du Salut. It may be a **BEAUTIFUL ISLAND**, but it's also home to the world's worst **PENAL COLONIES**.

BEHIND THE BARS

ALSO KNOWN AS:	The Green Hell
LOCATED IN:	French Guiana in South America
OPERATIONAL:	1852–1953
NUMBER OF PRISONERS:	More than 60,000 political prisoners
NOTABLE INMATES:	ALFRED DREYFUS (French artillery officer)

A penal colony is an **ISOLATED** place where prisoners are sent to be separated from society. Inmates called it the Green Hell. More than sixty thousand political **PRISONERS AND CRIMINALS** were held there from 1852 until 1953, when it was finally closed.

The journey to Devil's Island began on the docks of Marseille, France, where convicts were loaded onto ships bound for South America.

IN TRANSIT

They were kept in a temporary holding pen before the final leg of the trip to Devil's Island. When traveling by boat to Devil's Island, prisoners were held in **STEEL CAGES** belowdeck, eighty men to a cage. At the first sign of any disturbance among the men, guards would pipe boiling-hot steam into the cages. Upon arrival, **CONDITIONS WORSENED**. Prisoners were forced to strip naked and allowed to wear only a hat and shoes. In this state, they performed manual labor such as cutting timber, sometimes while standing in waist-deep water. Other times, they did meaningless labor, like building **ROADS THAT LED NOWHERE**.

PRISONERS ARRIVING

SOLITARY CONFINEMENT

By far, the worst punishment at Devil's Island was **SOLITARY CONFINEMENT**, in which prisoners were kept in complete darkness. Some were locked in pits in the ground with bars overhead. **UNPROTECTED** from the weather, the shackled men often sat in inches of rainwater. At night, **VAMPIRE BATS** would swoop in, bite the sleeping inmates, and suck their blood. Prisoners at Devil's Island called solitary the "devourer of men." And yet escape was out of the question: The **SHARK-FILLED** ocean and the thick jungle surrounding the colony served as a natural, **INESCAPABLE BARRIER**.

THE PRISON TODAY

Today, Devil's Island has been closed for sixty years. It is open to the public and tourists, who explore the **DECAYING** buildings and peer into the **CRUMBLING** cells.

A CELL BLOCK

PRISON CLOTHING

For most of history, prisoners wore the clothes they had on when they were taken to jail. They were rarely allowed to wash or replace these clothes. In the nineteenth century, as prisons became more regulated, prisoners were dressed in black-and-white-striped **UNIFORMS**. These uniforms served two main purposes. First, on an emotional level, uniforms made prisoners feel like prisoners and encouraged a sense of shame. Second, on a practical level, the uniforms made prisoners easy to spot if they ever attempted to escape. At various times in the twentieth century, prisoners wore jackets and gray, green, or brown cloth pants. Today, prisoners wear any number of different uniforms, depending on the prison. Some wear **ORANGE** one-piece jumpsuits, especially when being transported, so they are more **VISIBLE**. Prisoners in California wear denim-blue pants, shirts, and jackets. In Florence, Colorado, maximum-security prisoners wear khaki shirts and pants. In Cleveland, prisoners have to wear pink shirts and yellow-and-white-striped pants for **MAXIMUM VISIBILITY**.

FREMANTLE PRISON

Seventy-five English prisoners docked in Australia on June 1, 1850, surprising the residents of the nearby colony. Although they had requested British **CONVICTS** to perform skilled labor, the ship carrying the prisoners arrived without advance notice!

BEHIND THE BARS

ALSO KNOWN AS:	Fremantle Gaol
LOCATED IN:	The Terrace, Fremantle, in Western Australia
OPERATIONAL:	1855–1991
NUMBER OF PRISONERS:	Before they stopped transporting inmates, 9,700 prisoners were transported to Fremantle.
NOTABLE INMATES:	BRENDEN ABBOTT (bank robber), BON SCOTT (former lead singer of AC/DC)

The **PRISONERS** were immediately put to work constructing their own prison. They **quarried** limestone by hand and eventually built a main cell block, a gatehouse, high perimeter walls, a hospital, workshops, cookhouse, bakery, laundry, and six residences for high-ranking officers.

DAILY LIFE

The gigantic Fremantle Prison has housed just about every type of prisoner imaginable over its 120-year history: convicted felons, illegal immigrants, prisoners of war, and political prisoners. The conditions were harsh: Inmates worked ten hours a day while wearing leg irons and **SHACKLES**, which bruised and wore away the skin. They were beaten and whipped when they disobeyed the guards. Sometimes they were locked in **WINDOWLESS CELLS**, where they lost track of time in the darkness.

LEG IRON SHACKLES

INESCAPABLE

Some did try to **ESCAPE**, but they rarely succeeded—the climate and wild animals of Western

Australia were too harsh and **DANGEROUS**. The land outside the colony was almost entirely unsettled, and miles of thick outback bush lay between prisoners and the ocean. In fact, the land around Fremantle was so difficult to travel through that officials called Fremantle a **PRISON WITHIN A PRISON**.

THE END

In 1964, an inmate was hanged at Fremantle, making him one of the last people to be executed in the country of Australia. Fremantle **CLOSED** in 1991, ending its legacy as one of the largest convict prisons in the world.

PRISONERS AT WORK

FLEEING FROM FREMANTLE: THE STORY OF THE SHARK BAY ESCAPE

In 1859, five inmates from Fremantle were sent to perform manual labor in town. However, they used this opportunity to escape and **DISAPPEAR** into the bush. Police rounded up native people, called Aborigines, to help track the convicts through the wilderness. Amazingly, the convicts next sneaked past the lookout master and **STOLE** a dinghy—a small boat not meant for open-sea sailing. They rowed to a small island, where they stole a larger boat and **SET OUT TO SEA**.

At this point, the escapees had a bit of **LUCK**: As they were rowing north, out to sea, they found the police boat was tied up, ready to carry the governor out to his vacation site. By the time the police got back to their boat, the convicts had a head start.

For five hundred miles, the men endured heat, wind, and huge ocean waves. When the police finally managed to capture the **fugitives**, they found that only four of the five were alive; the fifth had been murdered by his comrades. His crime? He had taken more than his share of drinking water.

OHIO STATE REFORMATORY

When constuction began on the Ohio State Reformatory on November 4, 1886, the people of Mansfield, Ohio, **CHEERED**, and the newspaper headline declared it MANSFIELD'S GREATEST DAY. The city had campaigned to be the site of the reformatory, expecting it would bring jobs and

BEHIND THE BARS

ALSO KNOWN AS:	Mansfield Reformatory
LOCATED IN:	Mansfield, Ohio
OPERATIONAL:	1896–1990
NUMBER OF PRISONERS:	155,000 during the time the prison was open
NOTABLE INMATES:	HENRY BAKER (a member of the Great Brinks robbery gang)

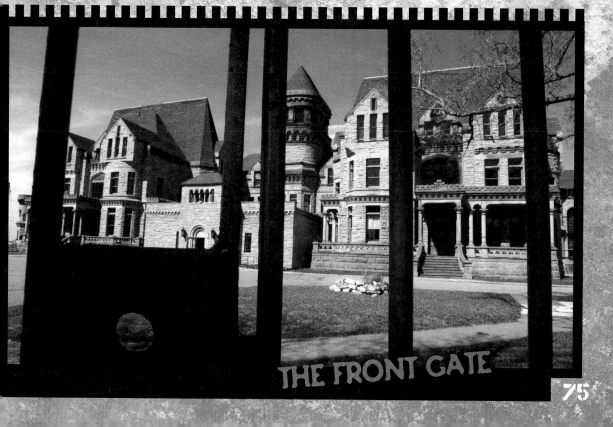

THE FRONT GATE

BOYS TO MEN

The Mansfield Reformatory, as it was sometimes called, was meant to serve as a transition between **JUVENILE DETENTION** and the Ohio Penitentiary. During its first year, **150 BOYS** moved in, most of whom were first-time offenders. Eventually, the reformatory would house 155,000 boys and men during the one hundred years it was in operation. Built on the site of a former Civil War camp, the grand architecture was designed to **INTIMIDATE** prisoners and inspire regret. It has been called Dracula's Castle, and many contemporary film and television producers have been drawn to its dramatic towers, archways, and echoing chambers. Portions of the 1994 Oscar-nominated film *The Shawshank Redemption* were shot there. The prison has one of the largest freestanding cell blocks in the world, which rises six stories high.

INSIDE A CELL

PRISON GHOSTS

Ghost legends abound at the Mansfield Reformatory. Visitors have reported **DOORS SLAMMING**, the feeling of being pushed or scratched, and **STRANGE VOICES** that cry out from empty cells. The museum runs a thriving ghost-hunting business, and paranormal investigators come from all over the country to investigate these reports. Some bring special equipment for detecting ghosts. **GHOST HUNTERS** have reported "cold spots" and equipment malfunctions—which paranormal believers take to mean that **SPIRIT ENERGY** is present. Some say the former prison warden's voice can be heard in the abandoned prison office. His wife's perfume can still be smelled in her private bathroom—or so the story goes.

During the prison ghost hunts, guides sometimes use a device called a dowsing rod to talk to spirits. A dowsing rod looks like two long, L-shaped wires. The guide holds them in his or her hands and asks questions of a ghost nearby. According to the guide, the movement of the wires indicates if the ghost has responded yes or no.

Is Mansfield really haunted by the spirits of those who died there? Or do the visitors have an overactive imagination and a desire for connection with the **SPIRIT WORLD?**

SQUIRREL CAGE JAIL

Imagine a series of cages that **SPIN** like a giant lazy Susan, with metal bars rising three stories high. Are these cages for lab animals? A place for keeping **ZOO CREATURES**? No.

WARDEN TURNING CRANK

BEHIND THE BARS

ALSO KNOWN AS:	Pottawattamie County Jail
LOCATED IN:	Council Bluffs, Iowa
OPERATIONAL:	1885–1969
NUMBER OF PRISONERS:	Three stories of the prison each held ten pie-shaped cells for prisoners.
NOTABLE INMATES:	The first superintendent of the jail, J.M. CARTER, is said to haunt the prison!

THE REVOLVING CELLS

This was a place for keeping humans—the historic Pottawattamie County Squirrel Cage Jail in Council Bluffs, Iowa. The jail was built like a **REVOLVING DOOR**: three stories of ten steel cagelike cells revolve around a central axis. The cells are **PIE SHAPED**, and together form a big cylinder, like a larger cage. The jailer could operate a hand crack that **ROTATED THE CELLS** until they lined up with a door opening.

PAY THE PRICE

The building also contained offices, a kitchen, and quarters for women, as well as an apartment for the jailer and his family on the fourth floor—though none of those rooms revolved.

The Squirrel Cage Jail, which cost $30,000 to build, was invented in 1881 by two Indianapolis men, who received a patent for its design. Their goal, they declared on their patent application, was to reduce personal contact between the prisoners and the jailer. They wanted to allow the jailer to be able to pay minimal attention while still providing **MAXIMUM SECURITY**. One jailer and one deputy should be able to control the entire jail.

The Squirrel Cage Jail is the only **THREE-STORY REVOLVING JAIL** ever built, though there are two other revolving jails still standing: a one-story jail in Gallatin, Missouri, and a two-story jail in Crawfordsville, Indiana. The Squirrel Cage doesn't rotate anymore, but it still looks much as it did when it closed in 1969. Today, visitors can tour the jail.

PIE-SHAPED CELL

PRISON JOBS

Most inmates in modern prisons don't spend all day in their cells. Many prisoners, especially those who are considered minimum security, work at jobs within the prison. Some might help to run different parts of the prison itself: **COOK** or clean in the kitchens, **SERVE** in the cafeterias, check out and **SHELVE BOOKS** in the prison library, or **DO LAUNDRY**. Some prisoners do jobs that serve the outside community, such as picking up trash by the road or working on a prison-run farm. Others might help with **CONSTRUCTION** of prison buildings. Sometimes, inmates work at manufacturing jobs right in the prison itself, such as **SEWING** T-shirts, making license plates, or building office furniture. These jobs help keep the prisoners busy and often help them develop new skills that they may use when they are released.

KOLYMA GULAG CAMP

Imagine performing **HARD LABOR** outdoors in little clothing, day after day, year after year, in one of the **COLDEST** places on earth. That was life in the Gulag **FORCED** labor camp at Kolyma.

BEHIND THE BARS

ALSO KNOWN AS:	The Gulag
LOCATED IN:	Siberia, Russia
OPERATIONAL:	1929–1953
NUMBER OF PRISONERS:	More than 18 million people were imprisoned at Kolyma while it was used as a labor camp.
NOTABLE INMATES:	MIKHAIL KRAVCHUK (Ukrainian mathematician)

The Soviet government established the Gulag, a **SYSTEM** of hard labor camps to **PUNISH** and imprison convicted criminals, petty lawbreakers, intellectuals, and prisoners of war.

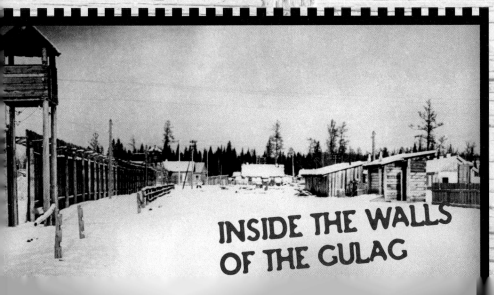

INSIDE THE WALLS
OF THE GULAG

THE CAMPS

The Gulag camps were established under the rule of Joseph Stalin, and flourished during the 1930s and 1940s, with many camps closing or easing conditions somewhat after Stalin's death in 1953. Kolyma was known as the **HARSHEST** of these camps.

PRISONERS MINING GOLD

LIFE AT KOLYMA

Kolyma was in Siberia—one of the **COLDEST** inhabited places on earth. This Gulag camp was so remote that it couldn't be reached over land. Prisoners were sent by train to the Pacific coast, where they

INMATES CUTTING DOWN TREES

waited for the rivers to thaw, then they journeyed inland past Japan, and up the Kolyma River to the camp. The trip was **BRUTAL**, and many died along the way.

Prisoners in the Kolyma camp performed hard labor up to fifteen hours a day, hacking at the frozen ground with pickaxes, or cutting down trees. They mined coal, gold, and copper by hand, inhaling dangerous fumes. In unheated, crowded **barracks**, prisoners were given little more than soup and bread to eat, and many experienced slow starvation.

There were fences around Kolyma, but they were not necessary. Nature's extreme cold was stronger than any man-made barrier. Prisoners joked darkly that Kolyma was a place where twelve months of the year were winter, and all the rest were summer.

TODAY

The number of prisoners in the camps gradually declined in the 1970s to fewer than ten thousand. The very last prisoners were released in the 1990s. Today, the Gulag camp at Kolyma is in **RUINS**, with only rusting tools and **ROTTING** fence posts remaining to remind us of the people who **SUFFERED** there.

THE SOLDIERS' BARRACKS

WHO WAS SENTENCED TO THE GULAG?

From 1929 to 1953, historians estimate that eighteen million people passed through the Soviet Gulag. These included people from all ethnic groups, nationalities, and religions—**NO ONE WAS EXCLUDED**. The government used the people in the labor camps to do large-scale labor projects, such as mining, so it was in their interest to send as many people to the camps as possible. Those who opposed the Soviet government were sent, alongside dangerous criminals.

INNOCENT PEOPLE also could be arrested and sent to the camps for even the mere suspicion of treason. Men and women could be sent for crimes as small as stealing bread from a restaurant, or even simply missing work without an excuse. The accused would be convicted in a five-minute trial, and then sentenced to years in the hard labor camps of the Gulag.

ALCATRAZ

Alcatraz, also known as **THE ROCK**, was operational for only thirty years, between 1934 and 1963. But this prison, which was built on an **ISLAND** in San Francisco Bay, is known best as the prison that housed Al Capone and other famous **GANGSTERS**.

CELL BLOCK

BEHIND THE BARS

ALSO KNOWN AS:	The Rock, Alcatraz Federal Penitentiary
LOCATED IN:	San Francisco Bay, California
OPERATIONAL:	1934–1963
NUMBER OF PRISONERS:	Approximately 1,500 prisoners over thirty years
NOTABLE INMATES:	AL CAPONE (gangster), ROBERT STROUD ("The Birdman of Alcatraz"), GEORGE "MACHINE GUN KELLY" BARNES (gangster), BUMPY JOHNSON (mob boss)

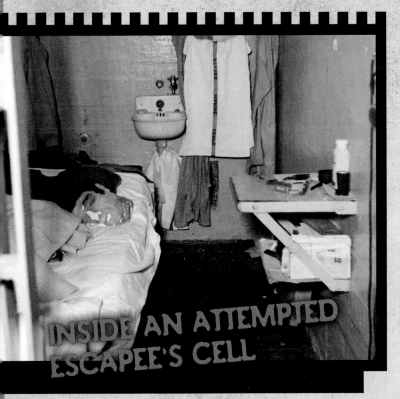

INSIDE AN ATTEMPTED ESCAPEE'S CELL

Alcatraz was a military prison from 1861 until 1933, when it became a federal prison. The population was strictly **MAXIMUM–SECURITY** prisoners, such as people who caused trouble in or tried to escape from other prisons.

THE ROCK

The island itself is a **barren** rock, with no natural water or vegetation. **ESCAPE** from Alcatraz was difficult, if not **IMPOSSIBLE**, and yet fourteen attempts were made over its thirty-year history. Some inmates were captured, others drowned. There were no sharks in the water around the prison, as many believed, but the water was extremely cold. It was thought no one could survive the swim.

Officers' Row Gardens

Main Road Landscape

EAST ROAD

BUILDING 64

DOCK

RECREATION YARD

CELLHOUSE

RESTROOMS

WARDEN'S HOUSE (RUINS)

West Side Gardens Greenhouse (ruins)

WEST ROAD

West Lawn

LIGHTHOUSE

Garden Shed

PARADE GROUND

MAP OF ALCATRAZ

DAILY LIFE

Alcatraz is perhaps one of the most **FAMOUS PRISONS** in popular culture. In reality, however, the conditions there were better than in many other prisons at the time. Alcatraz was never filled to capacity, much less overcrowded. Only one man was kept in each **CELL**, which was unusual for this period. Each day's structured routine was intended to control the population and to teach them to **FOLLOW RULES**. Prisoners were not tortured, and they were adequately fed, clothed, and given medical care.

LOOKOUT TOWER

MILITARY PRISON TO NATIONAL PARK

Alcatraz's operational costs were three times greater than any other federal prison. Every supply, including water and food, had to be ferried by boat from the mainland. Because of these costs, the government **CLOSED** Alcatraz after only three decades. Today, it lives on as a **NATIONAL PARK**, where visitors can explore the empty cells and listen to tour guides' tales.

THE LAST INMATES HELD AT ALCATRAZ BEING TRANSFERRED TO OTHER PRISONS

FAMOUS PRISONERS AT ALCATRAZ

Alcatraz is legendary, not just for its unique location but also for its famous prisoners: The 1930s gangster **GEORGE "MACHINE GUN KELLY" BARNES** was one of the most famous criminals of the Prohibition era—the period in the United States when alcohol was outlawed. After years spent smuggling liquor, Kelly and his wife kidnapped a wealthy businessman and held him for ransom. Kelly was eventually arrested and sent to the Rock in 1934. A more recent gangster, **JAMES "WHITEY" BULGER**, cycled through Alcatraz after he committed a series of bank robberies and was sentenced to twenty-five years in federal prison in 1956. Bulger was convicted of eleven murders in 2013, and was given two life sentences.

Alcatraz was also home to oddball inmates, such as convicted murderer **ROBERT STROUD**, otherwise known as the **"BIRDMAN OF ALCATRAZ."** Beginning in 1942, Stroud spent seventeen years in the prison after spending three decades at another federal prison. During his lifelong incarceration, Stroud bred and studied canaries in his cells, eventually writing two books on the birds and even concocting medicines to treat their diseases.

HOA LO PRISON

"I was at the Hanoi Hilton." That's how American prisoners of war (POWs) sarcastically referred to the Hoa Lo Prison in Hanoi, Vietnam. During the Vietnam War, American **POWS** were sent to the isolated and brutal Hoa Lo, where they were often beaten, shackled, and kept in **SOLITARY CONFINEMENT**.

BEHIND THE BARS

ALSO KNOWN AS: the Hanoi Hilton

LOCATED IN: Hanoi, Vietnam

OPERATIONAL: 1964–1973 as a prison for American POWs

NUMBER OF PRISONERS: 2,000 inmates in 1954 alone

NOTABLE INMATES: JOHN MCCAIN (senator, Republican candidate for the 2008 presidential election), NGUYỄN CHÍ THIỆN (Vietnamese activist and poet), JAMES STOCKDALE (vice presidential candidate)

PRISON CELL

This treatment was a strategy designed to force prisoners to **REVEAL** American war **SECRETS**. The POWs were kept in isolation but would secretly talk to one another through cracks under the doors, or **TAP CODES** on the walls to communicate.

THE TRUE STORY

One famous former inmate of Hoa Lo is US Senator **JOHN McCAIN**, who was held there after his plane was shot down in 1967. He recalls that his cell was six feet by three feet and he slept on a mattress stuffed with straw.

In spite of the **TERRIBLE CONDITIONS** at Hoa Lo, the Vietnamese government stated publicly that the soldiers were treated well. The government tried hard to control the world's understanding of life in Hoa Lo, and released pictures of prisoners eating a Christmas dinner, and claimed they were allowed to play sports like volleyball. They even forced prisoners to write public letters proclaiming the great quality of life at Hoa Lo.

Most of Hoa Lo Prison was demolished in 1993, and new buildings were constructed on its site. But one old wing remains, standing as a reminder of the **WARTIME** era.

PRISONER OF WAR: JOHN McCAIN

THE WORLD'S BEST PRISON?

If there is a good place to be imprisoned, Halden, a high-security prison in Norway, might be it. Prisoners at Halden have **SPACIOUS CELLS** with desks, carpets, **FLAT-SCREEN TELEVISIONS**, and personal bathrooms. Comfortable lounges are spaced out between every ten cells. Prisoners at Halden can play basketball, jog on wooded trails, scale the **ROCK-CLIMBING WALLS**, and take cooking classes—they even prepare their own dinner in small shared kitchens. Guards eat and socialize with prisoners to encourage good behavior. Inmates can have their teeth fixed in the state-of-the-art dentist's office, and **RECORD MUSIC** in the prison recording studio. Three Halden inmates even appeared on the Norwegian version of *American Idol.* Art and brightly painted walls help reduce the institutional feel of the building. And prisoners don't stay as long—the maximum sentence for any crime in Norway, even murder, is twenty-one years.

Many in the United States might feel that these luxuries serve the opposite purpose of incarceration. But the Norwegian attitude toward imprisonment seems to work! Released inmates in Norway are **reincarcerated** only thirty percent of the time, compared to American inmates, who are reincarcerated about sixty-five percent of the time.

ATTICA

The grainy photographs are **HAUNTING**: Disheveled men stand at gunpoint, hands on their heads. They have formed a wobbly line among trash, broken furniture, and heaps of ashes and dirt. This is the scene from the aftermath of the **ATTICA PRISON RIOT**.

BEHIND THE BARS

ALSO KNOWN AS:	Attica Correctional Facility
LOCATED IN:	Attica, New York
OPERATIONAL:	1931–Present
NUMBER OF PRISONERS:	2,150 inmates
NOTABLE INMATES:	H. RAP BROWN (leader of the Black Panther Party), MARK DAVID CHAPMAN (killed John Lennon), WILLIE SUTTON (bank robber)

THE AFTERMATH OF THE RIOT

The riot was a four-day uprising that occurred in 1971, in which the inmates were brutally **OVERPOWERED** in what was later called the "bloodiest one-day encounter between Americans since the Civil War."

RISING TENSIONS

THE INSIDE OF A CELL

Attica is a huge **MAXIMUM—SECURITY** prison in upstate New York. At the time of the riot, tensions were rising among the inmates. The prison was **OVERCROWDED** at double its intended capacity. Mail was routinely opened and destroyed by jailers. Prisoners complained of food that was **INFESTED** with **COCKROACHES**. But everything came to a head when George Jackson—a prominent African American activist—was killed during an escape attempt from San Quentin Prison in California. Thirteen hundred inmates rose up and took over Attica, holding hostage forty guards.

NEGOTIATION

They issued a list of **DEMANDS** to New York governor Nelson Rockefeller that included better living conditions and more opportunities to pursue education.

Over the course of **FOUR TENSE DAYS**, state officials negotiated with the inmates. In addition to their other requests, the prisoners wanted to be **pardoned** for their actions during the riot. The governor **REFUSED** this request and so negotiations failed. One thousand **NATIONAL GUARD** soldiers and police stormed the building, dropping tear gas canisters and **FIRING GUNS**. When it was over, ten guards and twenty-nine prisoners were dead.

POLICE WAITING TO ENTER ATTICA

RISE UP

But reports claimed that even after the riot was over, guards continued to **PUNISH** prisoners. This spurred a wave of prison **REBELLIONS** across the country. Later, some inmates and their families won a lawsuit against the state of New York for civil rights violations, and the governor and prison officials were criticized for how they handled the situation.

The Attica Prison Riot is often mentioned in prisoners'-rights discussions and as a caution against **MISTREATMENT** of the incarcerated.

PRISONERS DURING THE UPRISING

EDUCATION IN PRISON

You can't do a whole lot while you're in prison, but often, one thing you can do is go to school.

Throughout most of history, providing prisoners with an **EDUCATION** while they were incarcerated would have been unthinkable. It was believed that inmates were there to serve out their punishment, not to learn lessons. But today, most inmates in US prisons have not graduated from high school. Studies show that people who take classes in prison are forty-six percent less likely to commit a crime again after they get out of prison than those who do not take classes. Prisoners taking classes are also **LESS VIOLENT** while they were in prison.

In many prisons, inmates can take classes online or by mail. Some states, such as New York, offer live high school or college classes right in the prison, taught by certified teachers or professors. Students do homework, write papers, and take tests just as they would in a non-prison **CLASSROOM**.

SING SING

Sing Sing, the famous **MAXIMUM—SECURITY** prison in New York State, has been open continuously since its construction in 1828. Originally built from stone, it has been remade in concrete and metal, but Sing Sing's tough **REPUTATION** remains. Bank robber Willie Sutton spent time there, as have countless other convicted felons.

BEHIND THE BARS

ALSO KNOWN AS: Sing Sing Correctional Facility

LOCATED IN: Ossining, New York

OPERATIONAL: 1828–Present

NUMBER OF PRISONERS: About 1,700 prisoners at a time

NOTABLE INMATES: JULIUS and ETHEL ROSENBERG (alleged spies), LUCKY LUCIANO (mobster), WILLIE SUTTON (bank robber)

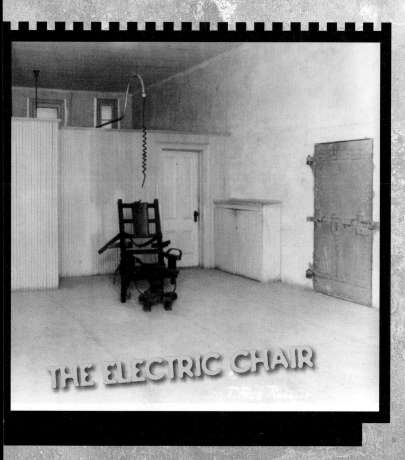

THE ELECTRIC CHAIR

THOMAS EDISON introduced the electric chair at **SING SING** in 1901, and since then, 614 convicted felons have died in "Old Sparky." It was also at Sing Sing that, in 1899, Martha M. Place became the first woman to be executed by electric chair.

In 1953, Ethel and Julius Rosenberg were sent to the electric chair, having been convicted of spying for the Soviet Union.

THE ROSENBERGS

DAILY NEWS

NEW YORK'S PICTURE NEWSPAPER

★★★★ FINAL

4¢

SPIES DIE IN CHAIR

BY HENRY LEE

Julius and Ethel Rosenberg, the A-traitors who for two years had tried to out-bluff Uncle Sam with the help of other Communists all over the world, finally were executed at Sing Sing Prison shortly after 8 o'clock last night.

The moustached Julius, his mustache shaved off, entered the death chamber first, at 8:04 P. M, and was pronounced dead, after the customary three electric shocks, at 8:11½ P. M.

But when Ethel followed at 8:08½ P. M, it required five shocks and she was not pronounced dead and already been unstrapped and she had already been McCracken

ordered the executioner to give her two more shocks. There had been some speculation that, near the end, they might crack and take advantage of government offers to save their lives by making a clean breast of their spy operation. There had been some belief, too, that they might die chanting the very Communist slogans which they had lived. But they fooled everybody—and their fellow Commies fooled them. Not one showed up in Ossining to carry on the demonstrations which the Commies have been staging all over the world for the

(Continued on page 3, col. 1)

LIFE IN PRISON

Through the years, Sing Sing has evolved. Now, inmates can earn a **MASTER'S DEGREE** from the New York Theological Seminary through an education program that involves studying almost full-time for one year. At the end of the program, inmates wear academic robes and receive their diplomas like any other **GRADUATE**.

INSIDE A CELL

CLOSE THE PRISON?

Perched on the banks of the Hudson River, Sing Sing is surrounded by the pleasant, upper-middle-class homes of Ossining, a community that is just a short train ride from New York City. So many New York **CRIMINALS** were sent to Sing Sing that the phrase **"UP THE RIVER"** has come to mean "in prison." Recently, residents of Ossining have asked the state to close this prison, which sits right in the middle of their town.

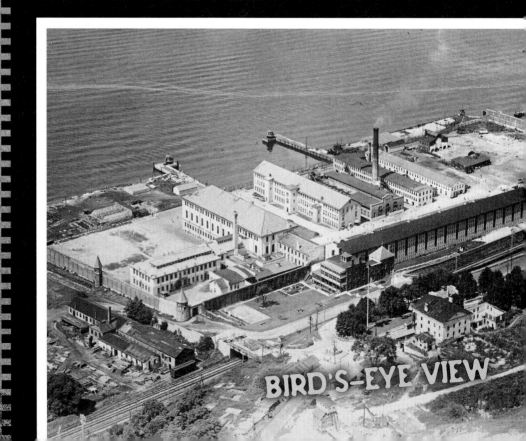

BIRD'S-EYE VIEW

LIFE IN A SUPERMAX

The ADMAX Florence Prison in Colorado is also a maximum-security prison, one of the most tightly controlled in the country—a **"SUPERMAX."** The layout of the prison is intended to be disorienting, so that inmates can't plan escapes. Prisoners are allowed no contact with one another for the first three years of their **INCARCERATION**. The most dangerous criminals live in cells that measure only eight feet by ten feet, have restraints on the beds, a tiny window, and a soundproof door. An attached cell for exercise looks like a cage.

ESCAPE from ADMAX Florence is **IMPOSSIBLE**. The compound's walls are guarded with twelve-foot-high fences of razor wire, studded with motion detectors, cameras, pressure pads, remotely controlled steel doors, attack dogs, and lasers that will set off alarms if tripped.

GLOSSARY

apartheid: a policy of racial segregation formerly practiced in the Republic of South Africa

barracks: a large building or group of buildings usually housing soldiers

barren: unable to produce crops

contemporary: belonging or occurring in the present; modern

dictator: a ruler who has complete control of a country, often by force

elite: a group of people who have more advantages and privileges than other people

excavation: a site where a large hole has been dug in the earth to search for something buried or to prepare for the construction of a building

flourish: to grow well; to develop and succeed

French Revolution: a revolution in France that took place between 1789 and 1799 that led to the end of the monarchy

fugitive: someone who is running away, especially from the police

irredeemable: not able to be saved

liberation: the act of freeing someone or something from imprisonment, slavery, or oppression

monarchy: a government in which the head of state is a king or queen

paranormal: very strange and not able to be explained by science

pardon: to forgive or excuse someone, or to cancel a person's punishment or other consequences

patent: a legal document giving the inventor of an item the sole rights to manufacture or sell it

philosopher: someone who thinks deeply and writes about the basic problems and questions of life

quarried: dug from an open pit in the ground of stone, slate, or similar materials

rebellion: armed fight against a government

rehabilitating: restoring to a former status or reputation

reincarcerated: to be imprisoned a second or subsequent time

revolutionaries: people involved in a political or social revolution

revolutionized: having brought about a complete change in something

treason: an attempt to overthrow one's government

CREDITS